COMFORT FOR THE WOUNDED SPIRIT

by

Frank & Ida Mae Hammond

SPIRITUAL WARFARE SERIES
VOLUME IV

The King James Version of the Bible is used throughout, unless otherwise indicated.

THE CHILDREN'S BREAD MINISTRY
P.O. Box 789
Plainview, TX 79073

COMFORT YE, COMFORT YE MY PEOPLE,

SAITH YOUR GOD.

SPEAK YE COMFORTABLY TO JERUSALEM,

AND CRY UNTO HER,

THAT HER WARFARE IS ACCOMPLISHED

Isaiah 40:1,2

FOREWORD

It is amazing how God works in our lives. Linda and I came to Frank's and Ida's home, as we had often times before, to receive ministry for ourselves. There was no mention of their personal needs during our phone call to arrange the visit.

Frankly, finding those we loved so much in a state of hurt and turmoil frightened us. What was happening to our spiritual mentors? How could we possibly help or give counsel to the ones who had taught and ministered to us so faithfully?

As we all prayed and shared, a glimmer of light came. The spirit-man had been wounded. This was not a demon to be cast out. It was the spirit of the person that needed to be healed. Who would think that one's spirit-man could be so wounded. But the Scripture is plain: "The spirit of a man will sustain his infirmity; but a wounded spirit who can bear?" Proverbs 18:14. Our excitement grew as the Holy Spirit gave us revelation and understanding. We knew that not only were we being healed, but, also, that we could comfort others with this same comfort. Here was a new area of ministry to help God's people!

Out of this vivid experience, Frank and Ida are writing to all of us who have been disappointed, hurt and betrayed.

Linda and I thank our Father for what part He let us have in this ministry to and with these servants who care so much for the Lord's flock.

In grateful love,

Stephen Bell

CONTENTS

Preface	vii
I. Let Hope Arise	1
II. Cause and Effect	5
III. How The Wound Occurs	9
IV. Symptoms Of The Wounded Spirit	23
V. Bible Examples Of The Wounded Spirit	29
VI. Comfort For The Wounded Spirit	45
VII. How Comfort is Obtained	49
VIII. When Comfort Is Refused	55
IX. Receive God's Comfort	61

PREFACE

Divorce! Trauma had struck our family. Without a hint of advance warning our daughter was caught in the throes of divorce. Sorrow and grief and shock consumed her and us. We battled tenaciously. Day and night we remained in prayer and spiritual warfare. One of us would pray the first half of the night and the other would pray the last half. The prayer vigil went on unabated. Days turned into weeks, weeks into months, and months into a year.

The heartache was constant - night and day. Every natural and spiritual approach to the problem was fruitless. The burden was crushing each of us. It was taking its toll emotionally and physically.

Ironically, we were working on the final draft of a book on family relationships, teaching others how to achieve Kingdom living for the family. The devil mocked us. How could we offer hope to others when there was failure in our own family?

One morning, while having our daily devotions, the Holy Spirit spoke to Frank's heart through a scripture we were sharing. We were reading in the Old Testament about the sorrow that consumed Jacob when he thought Joseph had been torn apart by some wild beast. His children came to him with words of comfort, but Jacob "refused to be comforted" Genesis 37:35. These words came ablaze in Frank's heart. He said, "Ida Mae, the Lord wants us to be comforted. God is saying to us that like Jacob we have refused to be comforted. We need to accept God's comfort."

That same day we received a phone call from Steve Bell, a pastor friend. He and his wife, Linda, wanted to come visit us for a few days — just to relax. When the Bells arrived they began to share with us a trauma that they had been going through in their church. The cause for their hurt was entirely different from our's, yet the effects upon each of us were the same: we were wounded.

The four of us launched ourselves into an intense Bible study. The Lord revealed that each of us was suffering from what the Word describes as "a wounded spirit". We ran every reference on "wounded spirit" and every related verse we could find. We discovered not only the symptoms of a wounded spirit, with which we clearly identified, but most importantly we learned God's healing remedy for the wounded spirit.

The study time led to ministry time. We ministered deliverance and healing to one another and to our daughter. Through this spiritual encounter our wounded spirits were comforted.

During the months that we had lain wounded, we had little spiritual motivation to help others, but after our own wounded spirits were restored, we were once again able to minister to others with confidence.

After having identified our own problem and applied God's remedy, it became apparent that many people needed the identical healing that we had experienced. Obviously, there are countless others who suffer from wounded spirits. We found the answer in God, and through His Word. It is out of our own affliction and subsequent healing that we are able to share with others the message: Comfort for the Wounded Spirit.

Chapter I

LET HOPE ARISE

> The Spirit of the Lord [is] upon Me, because He has anointed Me...to send forth delivered those who are oppressed — who are down-trodden, bruised, crushed and broken down by calamity. Luke 4:18, Amplified Bible.

These words from the lips of Jesus offer an oasis of hope in the middle of the desert of pain and sorrow. Jesus was quoting Isaiah's prophecy of a coming Deliverer and declaring that He Himself was the fulfillment of this prophecy. To a hurting world He was heralding the good news that He had come with a special ministry of deliverance and healing for all "who are downtrodden, bruised, crushed and broken down by calamity."

Let Hope Arise

God's Word offers hope for deliverance and healing. So often, deliverance and healing represent over-lapping needs. Listen to the word of the Lord through Jeremiah. First, there is the promise of deliverance from ALL enemies. There is no enemy too strong, too cunning or too evil for Christ to conquer.

> Therefore all they that devour thee shall be devoured; and all thine adversaries, every one of them, shall go into captivity; and they that spoil thee shall be a spoil, and all that prey upon thee will I give for a prey. Jeremiah 30:16.

1

"All they that devour...ALL thine adversaries, EVERY ONE of them, shall go into captivity." There is no enemy, no adversary, no demon that cannot be overthrown. Hallelujah!

Then, the promise of full deliverance is followed by the promise of healing. The emphasis in this passage is upon both the healing of diseases and the healing of inward wounds — especially the wounds of rejection.

> For I will restore health unto thee, and I will heal thee of thy wounds, saith the Lord; because they called thee an Outcast, saying, This is Zion, whom no man seeketh after. Jeremiah 30:17.

May God's promise of healing and deliverance bring hope to anyone who has lost hope; who feels that there is no remedy for his sorrow. Jesus is able to deliver you just as He has promised. One can come to Christ in absolute hope. Such hope is characterized by a confident expectation that something good is about to happen. Hope is "a way of escape" from whatever trial that comes, "that you may be capable and strong and powerful patiently to bear up under it" I Cor. 10:13, Amplified Bible.

The Bible defines hope as "an anchor of the soul" Hebrews 6:19. In other words, hope is to us what an anchor is to a ship: a stabilizing power. A strong anchor prevents a ship from being swept along at the mercy of every wind and every sea current. Without an anchor, shipwreck is immanent.

The calamities of life often cause one to abandon his anchor of hope which is the very thing that will stabilize him and see him safely through the raging storms. Like a jettisoned ship's anchor, abandoned hope is not readily retrieved. Nevertheless, it is essential to one's restoration and consolation that one's anchor of hope be re-affirmed. Dare to hope in Jesus Christ as Deliverer and Comforter. Dare to hope in His promises. Dare to believe that there is hope. Dare to hope that He will deliver out of despair and sorrow.

Before a man can accept the gospel of deliverance and healing, he must have hope. Therefore, hopelessness is the first enemy of deliverance and healing that must be vanquished, for hope is the prelude to faith:

> Now faith is the assurance (the confirmation, the title-deed) of the things [we] hope for. Hebrews 11:1a, Amplified Bible.

A person whose spirit has been wounded MUST hope in the Lord, for hope is the first step towards victory over sorrow.

Hope in Christ is not "iffy" but is "both sure and steadfast". Hope in Christ "cannot slip and it cannot break down under whoever steps out upon it" Hebrews 6:19, Amplified Bible.

> Now the God of hope fill you with all joy and peace in believing, that ye may abound in hope, through the power of the Holy Ghost. Romans 15:13.

The Apostle Paul prayed for the afflicted that they might be comforted of God. He reminded the Thessalonians that the One Who had given them "everlasting consolation" would also "comfort" their hearts in the midst of their present afflictions:

> Now our Lord Jesus Christ himself, and God, even our Father, which hath loved us, and hath given us everlasting consolation and good hope through grace, Comfort your hearts... II Thessalonians 2:16,17.

The words translated "consolation" and "comfort" are from the Greek word *paraklesis* (*para*, beside, *kaleo*, to call); hence a calling to one's side. In other words, comfort is found in association with a Person. The Holy Spirit is our Comforter (Parakletos) John 14:16; 14:26. Comfort is appropriated by a struggling pilgrim when, through hope and faith, he calls upon the Comforter to stand beside him and help him bear his load.

Inner Healing

The comfort that comes to the wounded spirit brings inner healing. There is a close relationship between deliverance from oppressing spirits and inner healing. A person in need of inner healing must be cured of an "infected" wound. Two things are necessary: the removal of the infection and the healing of the wound.

An inward wound can be compared with a wound in one's flesh. Suppose one cuts his hand. He will be wise to guard that wound from possible infection by applying an antiseptic. Should the wound become infected, healing is delayed until the infection is removed.

"Infection" can also complicate the inner wounds of brokenheartedness and sorrow. There is a spiritual infection that can invade such wounds through the entrance of "unclean spirits". Unclean spirits (demons) are like spiritual germs which infect an inner wound, but there is also a spiritual antiseptic which will prevent these unclean spirits from infecting a wounded spirit — the antiseptic is forgiveness.

Forgiveness is to an inner wound what hydrogen peroxide or isopropyl alcohol is to a wound in the flesh. When one forgives his enemies, unclean spirits are unable to infect the wound.

When complete and unqualified forgiveness is not applied in times of inner wounding, the wound is invaded by the spiritual bacilli of bitterness, resentment, hatred and anger. Therefore, in such instances, forgiveness and deliverance must precede the healing of the wounded spirit. Forgiveness of one's tormentors qualifies one to receive deliverance. Thus, when the festering spirits are cast out and the inner wound is cleansed, the healing balm of Divine comfort is applied, and the inner wound is made whole.

CHAPTER II

CAUSE AND EFFECT

A merry heart maketh a cheerful countenance: but by sorrow of heart the spirit is broken. Proverbs 15:13

What is the cause of a wounded spirit? "By sorrow of heart the spirit is broken." The Hebrew word translated "broken" is *nake*. *Nake* is elsewhere translated "smitten" or "wounded". The Hebrew word denotes a painful sorrow. This sorrow may be described as heartache, grief, anguish, misery, heaviness, desolation, despair, dejection, despondency, hurt, suffering or torment. When such terms appropriately label one's emotions, he will know that he has what the Bible calls "a wounded spirit".

These negative terms also describe the effects of a wounded spirit. The effects are inward — influencing the mind and the emotions. There are other effects of inner wounds which are outward and observable to others. For example, an inward wound is reflected in the countenance. A wounded spirit carries the opposite effect from a "merry heart" which creates a "cheerful countenance". The face reflects the condition of the inner man. If one is happy, his face will glow. If he is sorrowful, his face will be dull.

A merry heart doeth good like a medicine: but a broken spirit drieth the bones. Proverbs 17:22.

Here is yet another effect of the wounded spirit: sickness and premature aging. Dryness of bones is the opposite of a merry heart. Both happiness and sorrow bear upon one's health. Happiness has a healing influence; sorrow is debilitating.

The "merry heart" that removes the bandages and brings the cure, [literal meaning of the Hebrew word translated "medicine"], is not to be confused with the merriment offered by the world, for worldly mirth is superficial, sensual and carnal. It has no healing properties.

The word merry means "joyful" and describes the joy that comes through one's relationship with God — a joy based upon His goodness and grace. Literally, "the joy of the Lord is your strength" Nehemiah 8:10.

Strength gained through "the joy of the Lord" speaks of more than a mere feeling of security or even an inward renewal of physical and spiritual stamina. The Hebrew word for "strength" describes a strong and fortified place. This signifies that when a beleaguered saint seeks refuge in "the joy of the Lord" he is brought into a shelter from the battle where he finds safety from the attacks of the devil.

In application of this truth, what should one do when experiencing any sort of life trauma? For example's sake, let us assume one is faced with a life-threatening sickness. What must he do? First, he must maintain hope, for without hope he cannot remain happy. Where hopelessness dwells, the heart cannot be merry. Second, he must maintain a merry heart, for when his heart is merry he has a remedial power at work in his body. By rejoicing in the Lord, he finds refuge from the demonic attacks of infirmity and death.

Ida Mae's testimony confirms the truth that "A merry heart doeth good like a medicine". In 1986 Ida Mae went through a dark valley of physical sickness which required three major surgeries within ten months. During the trauma days of open heart and cancer surgeries, the Holy Spirit instructed her to be joyful. She literally sang upon her bed and kept praise music playing in her room around the clock.

In order to bind demonic kings and nobles, the Psalmist exhorts, "Let the saints be joyful in glory; let them sing aloud upon their beds" Psalm 149:5. This truth burned in Ida Mae's spirit.

In the face of death, she exhorted her family to remain happy. Whenever she saw any suggestion of concern in Frank's countenance she would say, "Be happy, Frank. Be happy!" Ida Mae's recovery was supernaturally short. The head nurse over her case was signally impressed by how quickly she healed and mentioned that she planned to do a special report on Ida Mae's remarkable recovery. We bear witness that God's Word is true: "A merry heart doeth good like a medicine."

> The spirit of a man will sustain his infirmity; but a wounded spirit who can bear? Proverbs 18:14.

The "spirit of a man" which can be wounded, refers to the human spirit of man. The Hebrew word is the common word *ruah*, meaning breath or spirit. In these passages, *ruah* is used as a psychological term indicating the dominant impulse or disposition which leads a man to a particular course of action.[1] The spirit of a man is his power of motivation. It is the thing that gives him fortitude to fight his way to victory.

Normally, the human spirit of a man can rise up and deal with the problems that come into his life. This is essentially a matter of will power. However, when the human spirit itself becomes wounded, then a man becomes incapacitated. He no longer has within himself the resources to meet the challenge at hand. He must now look to a Source outside of himself. His only help is in God.

The human spirit is like an automobile engine. As long as the engine is operative, the automobile can go places and the owner can accomplish many things. If the engine

---

1 "From earliest Heb. thought, ruah had various meanings, all more or less equally prominent...2. Breath...or spirit...the same mysterious force seen as the life and vitality of man (and beasts)...It can be disturbed or activated in a particular direction, can be impaired or diminished..and revived again. That is, the dynamic force which constitutes a man can be low (it disappears at death), or there can be a sudden surge of vital power". The Illustrated Bible Dictionary, Part 3, Inter-Varsity Press, Leicester, England, 1980, pp. 1478-1479.

breaks down, the whole machine and its entire operation is immobilized. The automobile and its owner come to a standstill. The engine does not have the capability to repair itself; it is dependent upon a mechanic for necessary repairs.

Likewise, if the human spirit is functioning well, one can rise up and deal with his infirmities and many other problems in life. But, if his spirit is broken down, or has been injured, he must look to a "Spiritual Mechanic" named Jesus to get him back on the road again. One cannot heal his own wounded spirit.

Chapter III

HOW THE WOUND OCCURS

Rejection

Any wound that causes sorrow and distress can be the underlying cause for a wounded spirit. Rejection is undoubtedly the most common of such wounds. Rarely does anyone escape the hurt of rejection. It seems that everyone we have ever counseled has confirmed having been rejected to some degree at one time or another.[2]

Rejection is so powerful that some psychologists may now be utilizing it as a means for "natural" abortion of unwanted children. On an air flight a companion of ours met a young woman who identified herself as the daughter of "a leading American psychologist". She related that her father has proposed a new approach to abortion. He advises that a woman wanting to abort her child, be instructed to verbalize strong words of rejection to the fetus. The woman reported her father as saying that sixty percent of such verbally rejected babies naturally abort! Thus, rejection becomes an instrument for murder. This report gives credence to the seriousness of the wound of rejection. It is powerful enough to destroy life in the womb.

This evidence of death through rejection is totally inconsistent with the claim that a fetus is only a blob of tissue. Does not this report substantiate the fact that a fetus is a living, feeling person — a being who can experi-

---

2 See: Overcoming Rejection by Frank Hammond, The Children's Bread, Plainview, TX., 1986.

9

ence the wound of rejection as well as the benefit of positive emotions? Such evidence reinforces our conviction that babies need to be loved and accepted from the moment of conception.

Think of the repercussions in the lives of children who manage to survive this abortion-rejection tactic. Many of them will grow up to be psychopaths. The number of psychopaths is growing at an alarming rate due to the increased incidences of rejection and abuse of children.

Charles Manson is THE example in our day of the social repercussions which can come from a rejected child.

> Charles Manson has been called the most dangerous, feared man alive...Manson always had a black side simmering just beneath the surface. When it emerged the horrible result was the Tate/LaBianca massacre. The two-day killing spree left 7 people mutilated and dead, including movie actress Sharon Tate.

> There is no better living proof of what can go wrong if the attachment bond isn't formed than Charles Manson. He was born... to an unmarried 15-year-old girl. His life was spent in a succession of different homes and with a number of substitute parents. Finally, his mother asked Indiana state authorities to take over his care when he was 12 years old. Since the age of 12 Manson has lived most of his life behind bars.[3]

In his own words Manson explains, "Rejection, more than love and acceptance, has been a part of my life since birth."[4]

Charles Manson was rejected, neglected and abused as a child, setting the stage for the conscienceless adult he was to become. Thus, we see that the repercussions of rejection can be far reaching — effecting not only the rejected individual but society as well.

---

3 Magid, M, and McKelvey, C. (1987), High Risk. New York: Bantam Books, pp.22,23.
4 Emmons, N. (1986), Manson in his own words. New York: Grove Press, p.24.

Betrayal

The Psalmist, David, speaks of the wound of betrayal.

> Yea, mine own familiar friend, in whom I trusted, which did eat of my bread, hath lifted up his heel against me. Psalm 41:9.

It was his "friend", his close associate, who betrayed him. Is this not always the case? It was certainly true of Jesus' betrayal by Judas, one of the chosen twelve.

> And forthwith he [Judas] came to Jesus, and said, Hail, master; and kissed him. And Jesus said unto him, Friend, wherefore art thou come? Then came they, and laid hands on Jesus and took him. Matthew 26:49,50.

Betrayal comes through the closest relationships in life. It is necessarily so. The wound always comes from those in whom confidence and trust has been placed. This is why the wound is so painful; it comes from a friend, or a trusted companion.

In life, the bond of two people in marriage relationship expresses the closest of ties. The prophet, Malachi, rebukes husbands who betray their wives:

> And did not God make [you and your wife] one [flesh]? Did not One make you and preserve your spirit alive? And why did God make you two one? Because He sought a godly offspring [from your union]. Therefore take heed to yourselves, and let no one deal treacherously and be faithless to the wife of his youth. For the Lord, the God of Israel, says: I hate divorce and marital separation, and him who covers his garment [his wife] with violence. Therefore keep a watch upon your spirit [that it may be controlled by My Spirit], that you deal not treacherously and faithlessly [with your marriage mate]. Malachi 2:15,16, Amplified Bible.

Marriage is a covenant; a covenant of companionship. Husband and wife covenant to forsake all others and be joined to one another. The marriage covenant is based upon mutual trust. Betrayal, the violation of covenant relationship, produces trauma and pain. No wonder God hates divorce!

Abuse

Abuse is another way in which the spirit becomes wounded. The abuser is usually one in authority whose God-given role is that of protector and provider. Consider the hopeless situation of a child whose parents either abuse him or permit others to do so. Where can such a child turn for protection and solace? He is trapped in a cruel world of hurt.

In the Song of Solomon there is portrayed the dilemma of one abused by her protectors. The Shulamite, who represents the Bride of Christ, is in search of her Beloved. She goes to the watchmen of the city, types of our spiritual guardians, such as pastors and other leaders in the body of Christ.

> The watchmen that went about the city found me, they smote me, they wounded me; the keepers of the walls took away my veil from me. Solomon's Song 5:7.

This passage reminds us that abuse sometimes comes from those who are in spiritual authority; those who are abusive to the sheep. Some of the most cruel hurts imaginable are administered at the hands of church boards, pastors and other church authorities. These spiritual guides are charged by God with the responsibility of helping others find a close, personal relationship with Christ.

When protectors become abusers, the wounded sheep are left in confusion, bitterness and despair. Many of them will abandon all involvement in the church. When unfairness and abuse is equated with the church, who wants to risk the possibility of further hurt?

Abuse can be physical, mental, emotional or spiritual. Inherent in the meaning of "abuse" is injury or damage. Through maltreatment a person is wounded. The hurts may come through:

1. **Reproachful language.** How untrue the worldly adage, "Sticks and stones may break my bones, but words can never harm me." Many emotional cripples have become so through an assault of cruel words. Words have great power. They have the power to heal and power to wound, power to bless and power to curse. "Death and life are in the power of the tongue." Proverbs 18:21.

As Christian counselors we are often prone to ask, "Where are the abusers?" For the most part we minister to the abused. Seldom does anyone confess to having abused others. There is great need for honesty. Wherever there is abuse there is an abuser. Interestingly, the abused usually become abusers.

In order to keep from becoming a verbal abuser, one must bridle his tongue. "Let your speech be alway with grace, seasoned with salt..." Colossians 4:6. At minimum this admonition signifies that our speech should be pleasant and uplifting.

Parents, be aware of how your speech ministers to your children. They need to hear words of acceptance, approval, encouragement and godly counsel. Sharp words that belittle, browbeat, criticize and demean will leave deep wounds in children's personalities. Husbands and wives, let your words to one another be "...like apples of gold in a setting of silver" Proverbs 25:11, Amplified Bible.

Unkind words are selfish words as are words of self-vindication, self-righteousnes and self-will. The Word of God exhorts us to prefer one another above one's own self and to honor one another. It greatly simplifies the recovery of the wounded when family members repent of their abusiveness, work toward genuine reconciliation and practice genuine agape love toward one another.

2. **Physical harm.** As concerning children, it is important to distinguish between corporeal punishment (which the Bible advocates) and physical abuse (which is never justifiable). The rod of chastening must be applied to a child's posterior in such way as to bring positive repentance and change. The potential abuse of the rod as an instrument of punishment is why the Word admonishes fathers, "Provoke not your children to wrath..." Ephesians

6:4; and again, "Fathers, provoke not your children to anger, lest they be discouraged" Colossians 3:21.

Rightly done, spanking a child conveys a message of love: "For whom the Lord loveth he chasteneth, and scourgeth every son whom he receiveth" Hebrews 12:6. A child knows the difference between correction and abuse. In the long run, abuse will bring negative and destructive consequences.

Anyone in authority is capable of physical abuse. Husbands are no exception. Many physically violent husbands would be in prison if it were not for their wives being too intimidated and frightened to bring charges against them. On the other hand, wifebeaters would become extinct if all husbands would

> ...love their wives as their own bodies... for no man ever yet hated his own flesh; but nourisheth and cherisheth it, even as the Lord the church. Ephesians 5:28,29.

According to a report given on the Christian Broadcasting Network's 700 Club, over 1.5 million cases of child abuse are reported to civil authorities each year. Upon investigation, only 60% of these reported abuses are proven to be valid. Still, this is an alarming number of reported abuse charges.

Consider how many cases there are which are not reported. So, child abuse is no small concern. Case workers produce pictures of children who have been burned on various parts of their bodies by lighted cigarettes, and others whose faces and bodies are bruised and swollen from beatings. Even though the outward wounds may eventually heal, the inner wounds remain. Deep scars are left in the personalities of the abused, and these wounds will remain until they are healed by God. They will not go away by themselves. A person cannot simply rise above such hurts in his own strength. The ministry of the Great Physician is required.

3. **Sexual defilement.** The extent of sexual abuse has been coming to the forefront more and more in recent years. In the past, most sexual crimes against children

have been kept secret within families. Now sexual abuse is a major topic of exploration and exposure on television talk shows.

It is generally conceded that upward of one third of females have been sexually violated either by molestation, incest or rape. At least one in five males has been molested or sodomized. These are alarming statistics when one realizes the far-reaching repercussions in the personalities of these victims.

The disintegration of family life is a key factor in the increasing incidence of the sexual abuse of children. Children, on the whole, are not as well protected as they once were. Broken homes, unwed mothers and two working parents require children to be cared for by outsiders. In spite of precautions, the stage is often set for child-molestation.

Too, the increase in child pornography plants seeds of suggestion in the minds of the perverted from which spring forth overt acts of molestation, incest and rape.

When people who are sexual deviates submit themselves for counseling and deliverance ministry, they should be questioned as to whether or not they, too, have been sexually abused. In our own experience, we have discovered that most sexual perverts have themselves been sexually exploited in one way or another.

Incest is not uncommon. As repulsive as it seems, some little girls are exploited by their own fathers, grandfathers and brothers. Again, judging from our own experience, the incidence of incest is highest with step-fathers, uncles and cousins.

Sexual crimes against children leave some of the deepest wounds and cause some of the worst repercussions in the personalities of their victims that we have found. Many of those who confide in Christian counselors have never shared these secrets with anyone else. This means that shame and fear is buried and suppressed. The inner pressure of suppressed emotions is devastating. It takes its toll on every facet of one's being.

What a relief it is for such persons to discover that they are not hopeless victims of past abuses. There is deliverance, healing and restoration in the Lord!

4. **Psychological abuse.** There are all sorts and degrees of mental cruelty. The silence of non-communication is a common psychological abuse. The oneness of husband and wife is strongly reliant upon healthy communication. When one spouse oppresses the other by refusal to talk, such treatment constitutes psychological abuse. The silent treatment is often used as an instrument of punishment or as a means of retaliation. The pressures of such abuse can create serious repercussions within one's mind and emotions, even to the point of mental, emotional or physical breakdown.

Abandonment

The human spirit is also wounded by abandonment. Much sorrow accompanies the pain of being forsaken. Abandonment is an intensified form of rejection. It can range in severity from neglect to desertion.

Horrible stories of child-abandonment appear from time to time in the news media. We hear of newborn babies being thrown away in city dumpsters and the waste receptacles in public rest rooms. Some infants are found left on the doorsteps of strangers. These extreme examples of abandonment are reminders that many children are totally unwanted. More commonly, unwanted children are given up for adoption or passed on in the family for someone else to rear.

It might seem that mere infants would be incapable of experiencing the wounds of abandonment. How can they know what is happening? Although these little ones do not "know" by the processes of reasoning, they sense danger and upheaval through their emotions. The demonic kingdom also takes notice, and these cast-out children are quickly seized upon by marauding spirits.

Jesus protected little ones from rejection and hurt. When His disciples were insensitive to their feelings and needs, Jesus intervened.

> People were also bringing babies to Jesus to have him touch them. When the disciples saw this, they rebuked them. But Jesus called the children to him and said, "Let

the little children come to me, and do not hinder them..."
Luke 18:15 NIV.

The same Jesus whose love protected these little ones also reaches out to the our wounds of childhood. Thank God for the healing love of Jesus!

A heart-rending case of child abandonment is related in an earlier book written by us. There we tell of a six year old girl whose mother and father were divorced and she was in the custody of the father. Repercussions from the wounds of rejection had made her impossible to manage. One day the father abandoned her in the mountains of Colorado. He drove away hoping never to see her again. Fortunately for the child, she was found by someone before she perished and was returned to the father.

In desperation, the father brought this little girl to us for deliverance. The demons in her manifested savagely, but the girl was gloriously delivered through the Name of Jesus. The father also received deliverance, and the follow-up reports on this father and daughter were victorious.[5]

The Heavenly Father takes special notice of those who are abandoned. God revealed this fact to David, and under the inspiration of the Holy Spirit he wrote, "When my father and my mother forsake me, then the Lord will take me up" Psalm 27:10. This promise from God the Father can be claimed by all whose spirits have been wounded through abandonment.

Some husbands and wives abandon their mates for other partners. Some blame the mid-age crisis, but God calls it yielding one's body to unrighteousness! Jack (not his real name) was one such husband. Yes, as is common, Jack rationalized his unfaithfulness. His private business had gone under financially. He could not find comparable employment. He felt that God and the church had failed him. So, he began to live a deceitful life. He started cheating on his wife. He and his wife had enjoyed seven years of good marriage. They had served the Lord together and had been active in church. Without any previous hint, he

---

5 Hammond, Frank & Ida, (1973), Pigs In The Parlor, Kirkwood, MO. Impact Books, Inc., pp.66-70.

suddenly announced that he wanted a divorce. The shock upon his wife was horrendous. She was left with a one year old child to care for. She went through every emotional shock wave imaginable. Thank God for her strong spiritual foundation. Her faith in Christ Jesus carried her through the storm. Thank God, too, for Christian friends and family who supported her. Thank God for deliverance and for the comfort of the Holy Spirit!

There can also be a sense of abandonment when a loved one dies. A mother whose grown son had died, said to me, "Parents are supposed to die first".

My (Frank's) mother felt abandoned by my father's passing. He had been robust and healthy all of his life. On the other hand, mother was weak and sickly. She concluded that he would outlive her, so she made all her plans for the future based upon that assumption. She prepared special food recipes for him to use after she was gone. A few months after retirement, dad had a severe case of influenza which led to a heart attack, and he went home to be with the Lord. Mother lived ten years longer, but she always expressed the hurt of abandonment. Father did not follow her plan for the order of their deaths.

There are many who have never recovered from the death of close family members. They feel deserted. They refuse to be comforted. Let such ones be pointed to the Heavenly Father, "...the God of all comfort; Who comforteth us in all our tribulation..." II Corinthians 1:3b,4.

Again, there are some who feel abandoned by God Himself. The scriptures are plain, God only abandons those who abandon Him. The Lord warned that when His people

> ...go a whoring after the gods of the strangers of the land...and will forsake me, and break my covenant which I have made with them. Then my anger shall be kindled against them in that day, and I will forsake them. Deuteronomy 31:16,17

The devil, the old liar and deceiver, tells many of God's children that, because of adversity in their lives, God has forsaken them. Therefore, a child of God can carry the wound of abandonment through belief that God has turned His back upon him.

God is merciful, gracious and forgiving. Abandonment is contrary to these virtues. Even though the Israelites in the wilderness were exceedingly rebellious and appointed a captain to lead them back into their bondage, Jehovah did not abandon them. The priestly Levites testified:

> But thou art a God ready to pardon, gracious and merciful, slow to anger, and of great kindness, and forsookest them not. Nehemiah 9:17b.

Has one forsaken God? Then let him return unto the Lord, and the Lord will receive him as surely as the prodigal son was accepted home by his father. Has one NOT forsaken God? Then be assured that God has NOT forsaken him. He can stand upon the promise given to Joshua, "As I was with Moses, so I will be with thee: I will not fail thee, nor forsake thee" Joshua 1:5. This promise is repeated by the writer of Hebrews.

> He (God) Himself has said, I will not in any way fail you nor give you up nor leave you without support. [I will] not, [I will] not in any degree leave you helpless, nor forsake nor let [you] down, [relax My hold on you]. — Assuredly not! Hebrews 13:5, Amplified Bible.

Sin

"By sorrow of heart the spirit is broken (wounded)" Proverbs 15:13. Sin produces sorrow; therefore, sin can result in a wounded spirit. There could be no clearer example of this than that of King David. He committed adultery and sought to cover up his sin with murder. But David repented. In Psalm 51 we hear him crying to God out of a sorrowful heart. There seemed no escape or relief from what he had done. He was tormented over his broken relationship with God.

He lamented,

"My sin is ever before me" v.3.

He pleaded,

"Purge me with hyssop, and I shall be clean: wash me, and I shall be whiter than snow" v.7.

He implored God's mercy,

"Cast me not away from thy presence; and take not thy holy spirit from me" v.11.

Yes, David was a miserable man; he was overwhelmed with sorrow. He could not blame another; His spirit was wounded because of his own sin.

True repentance plunges one into the depths of godly sorrow; God's forgiveness lifts one to the heights of Divine consolation. There is no greater comfort than the comfort of God's forgiveness.

When, through sin, men create their own beds of sorrow, they have no one to blame but themselves. This is exactly what God said to Israel through Jeremiah:

My people have committed two sins: They have forsaken me, the spring of living water, and have dug their own cisterns, broken cisterns that cannot hold water...Lions have roared; they have growled at him. They have laid waste his land; his towns are burned and deserted...HAVE YOU NOT BROUGHT THIS ON YOURSELVES BY FORSAKING THE LORD YOUR GOD WHEN HE LEAD YOU IN THE WAY? Jeremiah 2:13,15,17, NIV, emphasis mine.

Sin brings ruin, but repentance brings revival. God has made a way of escape from sin's misery and loss. He said to wayward Israel,

Return, faithless Israel, declares the Lord, I will frown on you no longer, for I am merciful, declares the Lord. I will not be angry forever. Jeremiah 3:12,13, NIV.

This is God's word to every wretched sinner, to every person ladened down with the guilt of sin, and to every man who suffers the consequences of his transgression. The very reason that Jesus died on the cross was to bear the penalty of our sin in His own body. Have you found the comfort of His forgiveness?

Calamity

Life's misfortunes is another cause for inner woundings. There are traumas that occur which cannot be attributed to judgments from God. Some "friends" who think they have all the answers, are quick to label every calamity a Divine judgment. Such were Job's friends, but Jesus taught otherwise.

The disciples asked Jesus, "Who sinned, this man or his parents, that he was born blind?" "Neither this man nor his parents sinned," said Jesus, "but this happened so that the work of God might be displayed in his life" John 9:3, NIV.

Jesus also raised the question as to the cause of calamity when he asked, "Do you think that these Galileans [whose blood Pilate had mixed with their sacrifices] were worse sinners than all the other Galileans because they suffered this way? I tell you, no!...Or those eighteen who died when the tower of Siloam fell on them — do you think they were more guilty than all the others living in Jerusalem? I tell you, no!" Luke 13:1-5, NIV.

When the space shuttle Challenger blew up, thirteen people perished, and their families along with the whole nation were thrown into shock and sorrow. Did this tragedy happen because those astronauts were more wicked than others? The obvious answer is "No!" It was simply a calamity.

There are natural laws as well as spiritual laws which govern our lives. Automobile wrecks, plane crashes and other accidents result when natural laws are violated. Two material objects cannot occupy the same space at the same time. Hazards are involved when space ships and airplanes fly against the law of gravity. Sometimes people get hurt and are killed and other's lives are affected.

A certain woman comes to mind. She and her husband had a good marriage and their home was in peace. One day the husband experienced a severe head injury in an automobile crash. His brain was damaged, and for years the function of his mind has been seriously impaired. This has thrown great stress upon the family. Why did this happen? It was a calamity. The devil will compound such situations with consternation. He will attempt to perpetually torment that family with the "why" question.

For years this precious lady has called us frequently for prayer and encouragement. After the Lord had revealed to us the causes and cures for the wounded spirit, we could see that above all else she needed God's ministry of comfort. We were able to minister to her in a new dimension of truth.

Comfort is the only cure for a sorrowful heart. Each of us needs to learn the source of true comfort and how to appropriate it. One never knows when he might need such comfort for himself.

Chapter IV

SYMPTOMS OF
THE WOUNDED SPIRIT

When one goes to the family physician with an ailment, the doctor is vitally interested in knowing the symptoms associated with the problem. Christian counselors function much like medical doctors. They listen to the "patient" recount his symptoms, then the counselor prescribes and treats accordingly.

Over the years we have listened to many hurting saints recount their feelings. Here are the ways in which inner wounds generally are identified by their symptoms:

Inner Rawness

Those who have sustained a wounded spirit often describe it as an inner rawness — like a bleeding inside the chest. They simply hurt and ache within. The pain never seems to completely heal.

Time usually brings some degree of relief from inner wounds, but this inner soreness is like a tender wound in the flesh which is easily re-injured by a simple bump or scrape, and the wound becomes fresh and sensitive all over again. It does not take anything more than a thoughtless word to open the wound afresh.

As a young boy I (Frank) was very active — always running, jumping and climbing. One day I fell on a pavement and scraped a patch of skin off my knee. In spite of mother's prompt attention in dressing my wound, it somehow became infected. This was before the days of antibiotics. Mom's favorite remedy for infections was coal tar salve. She would apply this black salve daily and put on a fresh bandage. After a few days a nice scab formed, and it appeared that the wound was almost healed. Then I fell down again, knocked off the scab, and reopened the wound. The healing process had to begin all over again.

This pattern of near healing and re-injury repeated itself for months before the infection was fully cured and the wound completely healed. This injury, partial healing and re-injury syndrome is the same pattern observed over and over with individuals who have been inwardly hurt by the words and deeds of others. As time passes, the hurt and its memories begin to fade. It would seem that the whole matter were now relegated to the past tense. THEN, something happens! Someone (often the one who caused the wound initially) makes a caustic comment and the wound is re-opened.

Recipients of inner wounds are usually quite sensitive to offensive words, threatening looks and unkind actions from others. Tears are usually very close to the surface. It does not take much of a "bump or scrape" to re-open an old wound.

Continual Grief And Sorrow

The wounded-spirited person is unhappy. Sorrow and grief hang like a dark cloud over his head. One is reminded of a character in the Li'l Abner cartoon strip named Gloomy Gus. Everywhere this sad little man goes there is always a black rain cloud over his head. Likewise, heaviness of heart cannot easily be pushed aside; it just lingers and lingers.

Joy is usually contagious, but the individual with a wounded spirit can be in association with happy, laughing people and their mirth will not penetrate him. He simply feels separate and aloof from all enjoyment. In fact, he may even experience resentment. He reasons, "What right do others have to be happy and free when I am so miserable?"

Hopelessness

Yet another symptom of the wounded spirit is hopelessness. There is no anticipation of things ever getting better. One's future looks completely bleak. He feels that he is in a cruel trap; there is no way of escape. Heaviness and a depression envelope him. He is sure that he will go to his grave as wretched as he is now.

In his emphasis upon the believer's bodily resurrection, Paul said that those who do not have hope in life after death "are of all men most miserable" I Corinthians 15:19.

The future must be faced with hope. The only alternative to hope is hopelessness, and hopelessness is characterized by misery and wretchedness.

In Ezekiel's vision of the valley filled with dry bones he was being shown "the whole house of Israel" who say, "Our bones are dried, and our hope is lost" Ezekiel 37:11. Indeed, life's adversities cause many to give up hope, and the loss of hope affects one's whole being. Whenever a person relegates his future to defeat, without reckoning on God's ability, he cuts himself off from the way of life. The path of hope leads to the healing of the wounded spirit with its restoration of joy and peace.

Inability To Trust

Trust is fragile; it is easily crushed. When trust is shattered it becomes like the fallen Humpty Dumpty. Who can put it together again? It is not impossible, for nothing is impossible with God. Nevertheless, great patience and perseverance are required. There must be a willingness to try.

It is bad enough for one to lose trust in another human being, but it is absolute tragedy when one loses trust in God. When people fail us, it is all too common for God to be blamed. The only way to comfort is through God, and the only way to receive God's comfort is through faith and trust in Him.

Thus, trust is like a bridge between ourselves and others: the thing that links us together. When trust fails, the bridge between us and another is destroyed. The lost relationship cannot be regained without rebuilding the bridge of trust.

The one whose trust of others has been traumatically or repeatedly violated often develops what can be described as a "closed spirit". A case comes to mind when a loving Christian step-father came into a situation where his wife's children by two previous marriages had been severely wounded by their own father and a previous step-father. Their little spirits were closed to fathers. They were unwilling to run the risk of further hurt. Insofar as we know, these children (who are now young men) never opened their spirits again to trust either an earthly father or the Heavenly Father. How tragic!

It is an extremely serious matter when one closes his spirit: especially toward God. Why? God is the only source of security and comfort. And one cannot receive from God apart from trusting Him.

Have you ever tried to get a little squirrel in the park to come to you and take a peanut out of your hand? You truly love the little creature and only want to bless him, but he doesn't trust you enough to come that close and receive his goodie. You are disappointed by the squirrel's distrust.

Don't you suppose God's heart is pained when His little ones are afraid to trust Him? The blessing of God's comfort is in His extended hand. It requires trust to receive it.

Agreement With Death

A wounded soul often longs for death. He sees his plight as a living death anyhow. The devil, whose objective is to kill, is alert to one's desire to die. He will fuel that thought and even suggest ways to achieve it.

Hurting people devise many ways to escape the possibility of further rejection, abandonment, betrayal and abuse. They may spiritualize their way of escape by pining for Jesus' return. They may escape into fantasy, denial, suppression, alcohol or drugs, but the devil offers physical death as the ultimate escape from the difficulties of life. If one listens, the devil will even make death seem desirable.

Any agreement with self-destruction or premature death bears the devil's hallmark. Jesus wants us to live and to fulfill our calling. The Good Shepherd has come "that they [His sheep] might have life, and that they might have it more abundantly" John 10:10b, brackets mine.

Chapter V

BIBLE EXAMPLES OF
THE WOUNDED SPIRIT

Remember, the ONE biblical characteristic of a wounded spirit is "sorrow of heart" Proverbs 18:14. As we search the scriptures we find several outstanding examples of men and women who were deeply sorrowful. Let us examine each one concerning the cause of their sorrow, the effects of their wounds and the remedy, wherever given.

HANNAH
Samuel 1:1-28

Hannah was a beautiful character. She loved God and had a good husband, but she was very, very sorrowful. Why? She was barren.

Hannah's husband, Elkanah, also had a second wife, Peninnah, who had borne sons and daughters. The family was devout in their worship of Jehovah God. At the appointed times of sacrifice, Elkanah and his family made their way to the tabernacle to offer sacrifices to Jehovah God.

Hannah was Elkanah's favorite wife. He showed his love for her by giving her a double portion of provisions for her sacrifices to God. However, Elkanah's favoritism provided no consolation, for "the Lord had shut up her womb". Nothing other than having a child of her own would make her happy.

To make matters worse, Peninnah added fuel to the fire. She was Hannah's "adversary"; the devil's advocate. As the family made its holy pilgrimage, Peninnah provoked Hannah, taunting her because of her barrenness. One can well imagine the cruel words that were spoken to Hannah. This was no single happening, but happened yearly. Whenever they went up to the house of the Lord, Peninnah provoked Hannah.

Hannah's grief was compounded by continual torment from Peninnah. She wept profusely and could not eat. The sorrow was taking its toll upon her physically as well as emotionally.

Now, Elkanah was sensitive to Hannah's problem. He did his best to comfort his wife. He said, "Why weepest thou? and why eatest thou not?" I Samuel 1:8. He couldn't understand why barrenness was such a problem for her. After all, he loved her more than ten sons, and he told her so. Shouldn't his love for her be enough to comfort her? Indeed not. She refused to be comforted!

On one of their visits to the House of God, Hannah was there in the tabernacle crying her heart out. Eli, the priest, observed her for awhile and decided she was drunk. Eli confronted her and advised her, "...put away thy wine from thee". Again, her sorrow was compounded. She had now been falsely accused of drunkenness by a man of God.

Hannah's sterling character comes to light. She responds respectfully to Eli:

> No, my lord, I am a woman of a sorrowful spirit: I have drunk neither wine nor strong drink, but have poured out my soul before the Lord. Count not thine handmaid for a daughter of Belial: for out of the abundance of my complaint and grief have I spoken hitherto. I Samuel 1:15,16.

We can imagine Eli's embarrassment. He had seriously misjudged this poor woman. What could he do to rectify the situation? He quickly gave her a word of encouragement:

Go in peace: and the God of Israel grant thee thy petition that thou hast asked of him. I Samuel 1:17.

As one reads these words from the Bible it seems that Eli gave Hannah a little "God bless you" word that carried no real depth of meaning. Perhaps we so judge Eli because so many hurting people have gone to their spiritual authorities and received only a little "God bless you" response. There was no deep, fervent intercession, not even an anointing with oil; there was just a casual word to "go in peace" coupled with a monotoned hope that God would answer her prayers. It seems almost as though Eli did not consider her concern all that important. He showed no inclination to agonize with her.

But Hannah was a great person. She listened when the man of God spoke. She considered Eli the mouthpiece of God. His words rang in her heart as personal prophecy. Whereupon she exclaimed, "Let thine handmaid find grace in thy sight". She left the tabernacle a changed person. The sorrow and grief were gone. Her appetite immediately returned and she was "no more sad".

What brought about this sudden change in Hannah? She did not yet have a child; neither was she pregnant. She had heard a "Thus saith the Lord". The Word of God had created hope and faith in her heart. As far as she was concerned, God had heard her prayer and her baby was on the way! Thus, she was comforted.

What have we learned from the story of Hannah?

(1) Why Hannah was sorrowful: She was barren.
(2) What the effects of her inner wounds were: She wept uncontrollably, could not sleep and lost her appetite.
(3) How Elkanah tried to comfort her: He spoke kindly, expressed his concern and assured her of his special love. BUT HANNAH REFUSED TO BE COMFORTED.
(4) How comfort finally came. She heard and accepted the word of the Lord. She then had hope and faith that the answer was on the way. She had accepted God's comfort and was sorrowful no longer.

DAVID

Psalm 55:4-23

The 55th Psalm is generally thought to have been written by King David on the occasion of his son Absalom's rebellion, and that the enemy who dealt treacherously with him was Ahithophel, David's counselor, who joined Absalom in his rebellion.

Absalom's attempt to usurp the throne, coupled with the betrayal of his closest confidant, wounded David severely. He laments,

> It was not an enemy that reproached me; then I could have borne it: neither was it he that hated me that did magnify himself against me; then I would have hid myself from him: But it was thou, a man mine equal, my guide and mine acquaintance. We took sweet counsel together, and walked unto the house of God in company. Psalm 55:12-14.

This is the hurt of betrayed trust: the heartache of broken covenant. It is the same pain that is felt by a spouse betrayed by his/her companion when the covenant of marriage is violated by unfaithfulness. David continues,

> He hath put forth his hands against such as be at peace with him: he hath broken his covenant. The words of his mouth were smoother than butter, but war was in his heart: his words were softer than oil, yet were they drawn swords. Psalm 55:20,21.

The wife does not suspect that her husband is having an affair. He outwardly berates other men in the workplace who cheat on their wives, declares that he is devoted to his wife and would never do such a thing. Indeed, his words are as smooth as butter, but he is a deceiver and within his heart he is a traitor plotting war. His words are like oil, pretending that all is well, but the sword of betrayal is drawn and will soon pierce her heart.

When the betrayal came, how did it affect King David? Let him tell us in his own words:

> My heart is sore pained within me: and the terrors of death are fallen upon me. Fearfulness and trembling are come upon me, and horror hath overwhelmed me. Psalm 55:4,5.

Where could he find relief? Oh, that he could find some way of escape from this shock and trauma. With eyes flooded with tears he stares out of the palace window. A movement within the garden catches his attention. It is a dove picking up seeds. Moments later the dove mounts on her wings and disappears into the distance. David pines, "Oh that I had wings like a dove! for then would I fly away, and be at rest" Psalm 55:6.

Thoughts of escape flood his mind. "Lo, then would I wander far off, and remain in the wilderness. Selah. I would hasten my escape from the windy storm and tempest" Psalm 55:7,8.

It is people who hurt us; usually those closest to us in relationship — family, community, work place and church. If it weren't for having to relate to people, we could live safely. When we are hurt by others we begin to react like the Psalmist. How we wish we could fly away to some deserted island, find a cave, pull a rock over the entrance and escape forever from all possibility of further hurt.

But we cannot run away. In reality, taking flight resolves nothing. God doesn't expect us to run away; neither does he expect us to live with the pain.

Jesus was "despised and rejected of men; a man of sorrows, and acquainted with grief: and we hid as it were our faces from him; he was despised, and we esteemed him not" Isaiah 53:3. What does the rejection and betrayal of Jesus mean to us? It means that he is qualified to be our Comforter. We need not flee to some uninhabited place in the wilderness; we must flee to Him who is our Refuge. We must cast every care upon Him who cares for us.

As a young man I (Frank) was taught by my father to love the Word of God, but I could not understand the Psalms.

These scriptures seemed to be written by men who were manic-depressives. In one verse I would read exhortations to sing, shout and dance before the Lord, and a few verses later the Psalmist would be complaining about how bad things were and how indifferent God was to his problems.

As I grew older I began to understand the Psalms. I could relate more readily to what they said. The writers of the Psalms never spare the truth. They tell it like it is.

In Psalm 55, David relates his beterayal and conveys to us how badly it hurt. But he also reveals to us where he found his answer: "As for me, I will call upon God; and the Lord shall save me" v.16. Out of his experience he counsels others: "Cast thy burden upon the Lord, and he shall sustain thee: he shall never suffer the righteous to be moved" v.22.

God is our Vindicator. We need not become judge, jury and jailor of our adversaries. "But thou, O God, shalt bring them down into the pit of destruction: bloody and deceitful men shall not live out half their days; but I will trust in thee" v.23.

What do we learn from the Psalmist?

(1) Why he was sorrowful. He had been betrayed by someone very close and in whom he trusted.

(2) How he was affected by betrayal. He was sore pained within; preoccupied with thoughts of death; overtaken by fear and trembling; and tormented by the horror of what might lie ahead.

(3) What he first thought of doing. He wanted to fly away like a bird or escape to the wilderness.

(4) What he did. He called upon the Lord. He made a strong faith confession: "The Lord shall save me". He laid down all thought of revenge, leaving the matter in the hands of God. His trust was completely in the Lord.

(5) The result. He was comforted: "He hath delivered my soul in peace from the battle that was against me" Psalm 55:18.[6]

---

6 Note: David's natural enemies are a type of our spiritual enemies. Though a host of demons assail us, the Lord will deliver us from them all. "God shall hear [us] and afflict them" Psalm 55:19, brackets mine.

JACOB

Genesis 37:33-35; 45:25-27

There was prolonged trauma in Jacob's life, and most of it came by his own misconduct, both directly and indirectly. One of Jacob's mistakes was showing favoritism to one of his twelve sons. Joseph was the apple of his eye.

> Now Israel [Jacob] loved Joseph more than all his children, because he was the son of his old age: and he made him a coat of many colours. Genesis 37:3.

Jacob's favoritism of Joseph made the other sons jealous.

> And when the brethren saw that their father loved him more than all his brethren, they hated him, and could not speak peaceably unto him. Genesis 37:4.

Joseph compounded his brothers' jealousy and hatred by bringing his father a bad report concerning them. Also, Joseph shared with the family two dreams in which his brothers, and even his parents, bowed down to him.

> And his brothers said to him, Shalt thou indeed reign over us? or shalt thou indeed have dominion over us? And they hated him yet the more for his dreams, and for his words. Genesis 37:8.

One day Jacob sent Joseph into the field to find his brothers who were tending the sheep. When they saw him coming from far off they conspired to kill him. Their plot was to slay him, cast his body in a pit and report that a wild beast had devoured him.

Providentially, a caravan of Midianite merchants was traveling by, and Joseph's brothers decided to sell him to these Ishmaelites who carried Joseph to Egypt to be sold as a slave.

His brothers shredded Joseph's special coat, dipped it in goat's blood and took it home to their father. Jacob immediately recognized the coat and assumed, "An evil beast hath devoured him: Joseph is without doubt rent in pieces" Genesis. 37:33.

Jacob fell into a deep and prolonged sorrow: "And Jacob rent his clothes, and put sackcloth upon his loins, and mourned for his son many days" Genesis 37:34.

Eventually, Jacob's sons and daughters grew concerned over their father's incessant grief. They

...rose up to comfort him; BUT HE REFUSED TO BE COMFORTED; and he said, For I will go down into the grave unto my son mourning. Thus his father wept for him. Genesis 37:35, emphasis mine.

Our daughter and we had been in grief for almost a year when one morning, in our daily devotions, we began to read these verses from Genesis. Frank's spirit was deeply stirred by the words, "But he refused to be comforted". He said to Ida Mae, "Honey, this is our problem. The Lord wants us to be comforted, but we have **REFUSED TO BE COMFORTED"**. This scripture verse sent us into an intense Bible study which ultimately led to our being healed of our wounded spirits.

Now, back to Jacob. Eventually Jacob, too, was comforted. How did this come about? Let us quickly review the events leading up to Jacob's victory.

During the years of Jacob's grief, his son, Joseph, was going through severe trials in Egypt; nevertheless, God's providence was still at work. The good fortune was that Joseph was sold as a slave to Potaphar, one of Pharaoh's captains. The bad fortune was that Potaphar's wife made sexual advances towards him. To his credit, Joseph resisted the temptation and fled from her presence, leaving his tunic behind. Obviously chagrinned, Potaphar's wife lied to her husband that Joseph had attempted to rape her, using his tunic as evidence. Joseph was thrown into prison.

Joseph, while still in prison, had an opportunity to interpret the dreams of two fellow prisoners, one of whom told Pharaoh about Joseph's ability. Joseph was then summoned to interpret two disturbing dreams in which God spoke to Pharaoh. These dreams, as interpreted by Jospeh, revealed to Egypt's king that there would be seven years of plenty followed by seven years of famine.

Joseph's ability to interpret Pharaoh's dreams put him in great favor with the ruler of Egypt. Joseph was made governor and put in charge of a national grain storage and distribution program.

When the years of famine came, the whole region, including Canaan, was sorely affected. Therefore, Jacob sent his sons to Egypt to buy grain. There they encountered Joseph who first tested their character and then revealed himself unto them.

Joseph sent his brothers back to Canaan to get their father and bring him down to Egypt to live.

> And they went up out of Egypt, and came into the land of Canaan unto Jacob their father, And told him, saying, Joseph is yet alive. Genesis 45:25,26a.

What good news! Was Jacob elated? No, he did not believe a word they said. He had long since reconciled himself to the conviction that Joseph was dead.

The sons further reported, "And he [Joseph] is governor over all the land of Egypt" Genesis 45:26b. This surely seemed preposterous to Jacob. In his wildest imaginations he could not conceive that his son was alive, much less that he was second in command to Pharaoh in Egypt. "And Jacob's heart fainted, for he believed them not" Genesis 45:26c.

"And they [the sons of Jacob] told him all the words of Joseph, which he had said unto them" Genesis 45:27a. Surely, a detailed report of all that Joseph had said would convince Jacob that Joseph was yet alive. His sons would have reported things that only Joseph could have recounted and made their report as convincing as possible. But in spite of all the evidence, Jacob remained in unbelief and was not comforted.

Now, Joseph had dispatched a caravan of special wagons to transport his father and his whole family down to Egypt.

> When he [Jacob] saw the wagons which Joseph had sent
> to carry him, the spirit of Jacob their father revived: And
> Israel said, IT IS ENOUGH; JOSEPH MY SON IS YET
> ALIVE: I WILL GO AND SEE HIM BEFORE I DIE". Genesis
> 45:27b-28, emphasis mine.

Jacob was finally comforted. But how did it happen?
What was the key? The wagons! How could that be? What
was it about these Egyptian wagons that influenced
Jacob? These were no ordinary wagons. They came from
Pharaoh's wagon yard. Undoubtedly they were made from
the best wood by the finest of craftsmen. They could well
have been carved with beautiful designs and overlaid with
precious metals.

When Jacob saw these "Cadillac" wagons he was finally
convinced that Joseph was alive. He urged his sons to
load the wagons quickly. He was anxious to get to Egypt.

These wagons typify the grace of God and all that God
has done for us through Jesus Christ in order to demon-
strate His love and to provide our salvation and healing.
Just as Joseph sent the wagons, God (by his grace) sent
His Son with provision for our needs, a message of hope,
a cure for our hurts, comfort for our sorrows and the
means to bring us to Himself.

The wagons bore witness that Joseph was alive, that he
had great compassion and that he also had authority to
deliver. The wagons testified to Jacob what the empty
tomb testifies to us. Jesus is alive! He reaches out to us in
compassion. All authority in heaven and earth is His to
heal and comfort.

The old, old story; the glorious gospel of our Lord and
Savior Jesus Christ, is the key to comfort for the wounded spirit. The gospel is the key to ALL our needs. But, in
the words of Isaiah, "Who hath believed our report?"
Isaiah 53:1.

Just as Jacob proclaimed in faith, "Joseph my son is yet
alive!" each of us must affirm by our faith: "Jesus is alive! I
will go to him before I die in my misery and grief. He will
comfort my soul". Faith is a key to receiving God's comfort.

Without faith it is impossible to please God, because anyone who comes to him must believe that he exists and that he rewards those who earnestly seek him. Hebrews 11:6 NIV.

RACHAEL

Jeremiah 31:15-17

The mothers in Israel (referred to by Jeremiah as "Rachael") were in deep sorrow. Israel had been at war, and many of their young men had become prisoners of war. There was no hope for these young men's safe return. Therefore, these mothers grieved over the loss of their children.

A voice was heard in Ramah, lamentation, and bitter weeping; RACHAEL weeping for her children REFUSED TO BE COMFORTED for her children, because they were not. Jeremiah 31:15, emphasis mine.

Jeremiah came to these women with a message of hope:

Thus saith the Lord; Refrain thy voice from weeping, and thine eyes from tears: for thy work shall be rewarded, saith the Lord; and they shall come again from the land of the enemy. And there is hope in thine end, saith the Lord, that thy children shall come again to their own border. Jeremiah 31:16,17.

Once again we are reminded that, "By sorrow of heart the spirit is broken (Hebrew, wounded)". The ONLY remedy for a wounded spirit is comfort. But, comfort can be refused. Hannah refused to be comforted over her barrenness. David refused to be comforted when betrayed. Jacob refused to be comforted over the loss of his son. The women of Israel refused to be comforted while their sons were in captivity.

For those with a wounded spirit the future looks hopeless. Therefore, the promises of God offer hope. "There is hope in your future, says the Lord" Jeremiah 31:17, Amplified Bible.

Hope is necessary for the healing of the wounded spirit. Hope in God and His promises is the first step up the path that leads to comfort. Hope precedes faith. "Now faith is being sure of what we hope for..." Hebrews 11:1, NIV.

THE PSALMIST
Psalm 77:1-12

The Psalmist is identified as Asaph, one of the leaders of the Temple singers. The Psalm begins with a cry out of the anguish of his soul, but we are not told the exact cause of his oppression. The thing that stands out in Asaph's example of sorrow is that he follows the same pattern of behavior we have found with Hannah, David, Jacob and "Rachael" when he declares, "MY SOUL REFUSED TO BE COMFORTED" Psalm 77:2.

Refusal to be comforted represents a mind set. The Hebrew word for "refuse" is *maan* which signifies "to refuse with a resolved mind, which cannot be prevailed upon by the means that have been used; figuratively applied to a wound that admits of no cure".[7]

When one stubbornly says, "I will go to my grave in grief", or, "I refuse to be comforted", he cannot be comforted. God does not violate the human will. One must choose to be comforted. The will of a man must agree with the will of God.

One without comfort is miserable. He may seek God fervently, as Asaph did, yet remain in distress:

> When I was in distress, I sought the Lord; at night I stretched out untiring hands and my soul refused to be comforted. v.2, NIV.

Both Hannah and Rachael wept bitterly before the Lord, but neither were comforted until hope and faith arose. Our own family followed the same pattern. We cried and agonized before the Lord, but we were not comforted. What is the lesson in this? One must do more than cry

---

7. Wilson, Wm., Old Testament Word Studies (1978), Grand Rapids, MI, Kregle Publications, p.344.

out to the Lord in complaint and self-pity; he must roll his burden upon the Lord, obey His counsel and accept His comfort.

Where could I go but to the Lord? The Lord alone is my Comforter. Jesus came "to heal the brokenhearted" Luke 4:18.

He was

> ...a man of sorrows, and acquainted with grief...he hath borne our griefs, and carried our sorrows...the chastisement [necessary to obtain] our peace was upon him; and with his stripes we are healed. Isaiah 53:3-5, brackets mine.

Jesus was beaten physically and wounded inwardly. He not only provides healing for our bodies but also healing for our inner man.

Oh, how miserable is he who is not comforted! The Psalmist lamented, "I remembered God, and was troubled" Psalm 77:3a. The very memory of God augmented his woe. Why did God let this trouble happen to him? Why hasn't God done something to alleviate his suffering? Why do his prayers go unanswered?

"I complained, and my spirit was overwhelmed" v.3b. The Hebrew word for "complained" means "an inward or outward expression of sorrow, on which the mind enlarges".[8] Who has not experienced this torment of the mind? When the mind is stayed on God there will be peace, but when it dwells on the problem there will be torment.

"Thou holdest mine eyes waking: I am so troubled that I cannot speak" v.4. This tormented soul is so perplexed over God's failure to act that he is unable to sleep or speak.

"I have considered the days of old, the years of ancient times" Psalm 77:5. The Psalmist now meditates on biblical history, searching for some logical or theological explanation to his dilemma. He recalls every Bible character who

---

8 Ibid, p.90.

went through trials. He probably spent extra time thinking about Job.

Then he reviewed his own past. There were some happy days. "I call to remembrance my song in the night: I commune with mine own heart: and my spirit made diligent search" v.6. The memory of God's mercy only intensified his consternation. Questions about God disquieted his spirit:

> Will the Lord cast off forever? and will he be favourable no more? Is his mercy clean gone for ever? doth his promise fail for evermore? Hath God forgotten to be gracious? hath he in anger shut up his tender mercies? Selah. v.7-9.

Finally, Asaph makes a quality decision to fuel his faith with positive thoughts. He declares,

> This is my infirmity: but I will remember the years of the right hand of the most High. I will remember the works of the Lord: surely I will remember thy wonders of old. I will meditate also of all thy work, and talk of thy doings. v. 11,12.

The remaining verses of the Psalm are positive. The chains of anguish are broken. What turned the key? He faced reality. He stopped complaining, feeling sorry for himself and blaming God. Instead, he decided to meditate upon God's mighty acts in delivering Israel out of Egypt.

When one meditates day and night upon the Word of God he will become as strong as a tree planted by rivers of water[9]; he will make his way prosperous and have good success.[10]

When one thinks upon the things of God, he is assured of the peace that comes through GOD'S COMFORTING PRESENCE:

> Finally, brothers, whatever is true, whatever it noble, whatever is right, whatever is pure, whatever is lovely, whatever is admirable — if anything is excellent or praise-

9 See: Psalm 1.
10 See: Joshua 1:8.

worthy — think about such things...AND THE GOD OF PEACE WILL BE WITH YOU. Philippians 4:8,9, NIV, emphasis mine.

The manifestation of comfort is the strength to rise above adversity.

Chapter VI

COMFORT FOR
THE WOUNDED SPIRIT

Thus far in our search for comfort we have examined three passages from The Book of Proverbs which speak of "a wounded [smitten or broken] spirit". We have also examined the accounts of five individuals who were in deep sorrow yet found comfort. Let us now review the spiritual principles discovered in our Bible study:

1. Proverbs 15:13 tells us the CAUSE for having a wounded spirit: "by sorrow of heart the spirit is broken [Hebrew: smitten or wounded]". Therefore, we can anticipate that persons who have experienced deep sorrow; by such hurts as rejection, betrayal, abuse (verbal, physical, sexual and psychological), abandonment, and repercussions from sin and life's calamities will likely suffer from the wounded spirit syndrome.

2. Proverbs 17:22 and 18:14 present to us some of the EFFECTS of the wounded spirit. There will be physical infirmities and premature aging. Joy and happiness will flee away. The hope, courage and strength necessary to rise above adversity will be lost. Therefore, one becomes so defeated that he must find help outside himself.

3. From each of the five Bible characters scrutinized we found they each had one thing in common: REFUSAL TO BE COMFORTED. Therefore, it is apparent that the ONE thing that heals a wounded spirit is COMFORT, and comfort must be accepted.

4. Before these sorrowful souls found comfort they were REQUIRED TO MEET SPECIFIC SPIRITUAL CONDITIONS: hope, trust (faith) and willingness to be comforted.

Since receiving comfort is the solution for the wounded spirit, three questions arise:

    (1)   What is the source of comfort?

    (2)   How is comfort appropriated?

    (3)   How is comfort manifested?

The Source of Comfort
God The Father Is Our Comforter:

> Blessed [be] the God and Father of our Lord Jesus Christ, the Father of sympathy (pity and mercies) and the God [Who is the Source] of every consolation and comfort and encouragement. II Corinthians 1:3, Amplified Bible.

Relief from EVERY sorrow and heartache has its source in God. He is full of mercy, pity and sympathy. God the Father is our Comforter!

> Who consoles and comforts and encourages us in every trouble (calamity and affliction), so that we may also be able to console (comfort and encourage) those who are in any kind of trouble or distress, with the consolation (comfort and encouragement) with which we ourselves are consoled and comforted and encouraged by God. II Corinthians 1:4, Amplified Bible.

God The Son Is Our Comforter:

Paul goes on in the context of Second Corinthians, chapter one, to explain that the benefits of Christ's own sufferings are fallen upon us. Therefore, God the Son is also our Comforter. That is, we are comforted by the full salvation which comes through Christ's suffering for us.

Paul himself had experienced the comfort that came through Christ's sufferings. While in Asia he was under such oppressing distress that he was utterly and unbearably weighed down and crushed to the point that he despaired even of life itself. In it all he learned a valuable lesson: not to trust and depend upon himself but upon God Who raises men from the dead. He had become so completely comforted that he could now face further peril and suffering with confident expectation of God's deliverance — whether in life or through death. He had the assurance that this same comfort would be experienced by those to whom he wrote.

Because Paul had experienced Divine comfort he could now confidently minister to others. He assured them that they also would be able to comfort others once they themselves had experienced God's work of comfort.

We further learn of God the Son's role as Comforter from John's Gospel. Jesus had been preparing His disciples for His crucifixion. He would be going away and they could not follow Him. The disciples became perplexed and sorrowful. So, Jesus comforted them with these familiar words:

> Let not your heart be troubled: ye believe in God, believe also in me. In my Father's house are many mansions: if it were not so, I would have told you. I go to prepare a place for you. And if I go and prepare a place for you, I will come again, and receive you unto myself; that where I am, there ye may be also. John 14:1-3.

God The Holy Spirit Is Our Comforter:

Jesus promised His disciples that after He went away He would send another Comforter:

> And I will pray the Father, and he shall give you ANOTHER Comforter, that he may abide with you for ever; Even the Spirit of truth; whom the world cannot receive, because it seeth him not, neither knoweth him; but ye know him: for he dwelleth with you, and shall be in you. I will not leave you comfortless: I will come to you. John 14:16-18, emphasis mine.

Jesus ascended into heaven, but this Holy Spirit Comforter will never leave us; He abides with us forever. In

Greek, the expression "another Comforter" signifies another of the same kind. The Holy Spirit is the same kind of Comforter as Jesus Himself. He is One called along side of us to bear our burdens. As Comforter, the Holy Spirit gives encouragement and alleviates our grief.

Where, then, is the source of our comfort? It is in God the Father, God the Son and God the Holy Spirit. The Godhead is our everlasting source of complete comfort.

Chapter VII

HOW COMFORT IS OBTAINED

One must first cease all attempts to comfort himself. Consider the following futile, but often attempted ways, of seeking comfort:

1. **WE MUST NOT SEEK REVENGE AND RETALIATION** against those who wound us. Esau was grievously hurt by his brother, Jacob. Jacob robbed him of his birthright and paternal blessing. Esau resolved in his mind that he would kill Jacob. However, he purposed to wait until his father, Isaac, had died, for the time of his father's death was at hand.

Esau's mother, Rebecca, learned of Esau's intentions and hastened to warn Jacob, saying, "Behold, thy brother Esau, as touching thee, DOTH COMFORT HIMSELF, PURPOSING TO KILL THEE" Genesis 27:42, emphasis mine.

Let those who have been wounded by the cruel treatment of others lay aside all attempts to gain any satisfaction through retaliation. Striking back at those who wound us is not our prerogative; this must be left to God's wisdom and justice.

> Dearly beloved, avenge not yourselves, but rather give place unto wrath: for it is written, Vengeance is mine; I will repay, saith the Lord. Romans 12:19.

Retaliation is not limited to violence and murder; it finds many expressions. Comfort sought through revenge will never be found. One must give up such foolish quests.

2. **SEXUAL AFFAIRS.** True solace is not found through adultery and fornication. A person who has been wounded by the unfaithfulness of his/her spouse may initiate a counter affair. Comfort is not attained in this way. We must give up our sinful and senseless attempts to gain comfort through our own devices.

In the seventh chapter of Proverbs we find the account of a young man out on the town. He decides to stroll through the district where the prostitutes hang out. Solomon calls him "simple" and "void of understanding"; meaning, easily enticed and seduced.

The harlot catches him, kisses him and invites him to her house for the night. She explains that her husband is away on a business trip. The husband has taken a bag of money with him, so she knows he will not be back for several days.

The impression is left that this woman was lonely. It seems that her husband was a traveling salesman. It is altogether possible that she was resentful of being left at home alone so much. She was looking for consolation.

The loose woman said to the young man, "Come let us take our fill of love until the morning: let us SOLACE ourselves with love" Proverbs 7:18, emphasis mine.

Sexual sin never produces genuine comfort. In fact, it violates the law of God and compounds one's problems. God says, "Whoever commits adultery with a woman lacks heart and understanding — moral principle and prudence; he who does it is destroying his own life" Proverbs 6:32, Amplified Bible.

3. **FOOD.** There are three passages in scripture which relate food with comfort. Indeed, palatable food for a hungry person provides legitimate bodily comfort. God expects us to be blessed through satisfying, nourishing food. "Bless the Lord, O my soul...Who satisfieth thy mouth with good things" Psalm 103:1,5.

However, there are some who seek comfort from life's miseries through over-indulgence. When they feel that no one loves or cares, they seek solace for themselves through food binges. In another extreme, some turn from food into anorexia nervosa and bulimia. This, too, is the wrong road to comfort.

4. **DRUGS.** Some seek relief through drugs. Whether alcohol, nicotine, cocaine, marijuana, heroin, tranquilizers or other substances are employed, no solution to sorrow, grief and heartache is found. Perhaps some would claim temporary relief through an inability to remember one's problems but at the risk of drug dependency and addiction. God's way is, "Casting all your care upon him; for he careth for you" I Peter 5:7.

5. **SUPPRESSION.** There are numerous ways of escape from emotional trauma. Drugs is only one such way. Suppression is another way. Suppression, in psychiatric terminology, means to conceal or withhold from consciousness. Through suppression one may push unpleasant and disturbing memories and feelings deep down inside and alleviate the pain they cause. Nevertheless, the memories and emotions, though submerged into one's subconscious mind, are still there. As a smoldering ember springs to life, these suppressed hurts eventually will make themselves known through either a physical, emotional or mental upheaval.

The remedy for a wounded spirit is not to be found in one's contrivances or psychology's ingenuity but in the Person of God. Therefore, the first step to receiving Divine comfort is to abandon every attempt to comfort oneself.

COME TO GOD:

1. **CONFESS AND ACCEPT RESPONSIBILITY FOR ONE'S OWN TRANSGRESSIONS.** Only the self-deceived place ALL the blame for their problems on the devil and other people. As God said to Israel through Jeremiah: "Have you not done this to yourself?" Jeremiah 2:17, NAS.

Whenever our suffering is due to our own sinful and foolish actions, we must repent and ask God and others to forgive us.

2. **WITH A FORGIVING HEART.** The hurts and injustices which we have suffered at the hands of thoughtless and cruel offenders must be forgiven as a pre-condition to experiencing God's forgiving love and favor. Christ taught us to pray:

> Forgive us our debts, as we forgive our debtors...For if
> ye forgive men their trespasses, your heavenly Father will

also forgive you: But if ye forgive not men their trespasses, neither will your Father forgive your trespasses. Matthew 6:12,14.

Does God actually require us to forgive heinous, repeated or continuous wounding by our enemies? Yes! And, God made no exceptions whatsoever.

> Then Peter came to Jesus and asked, "Lord, how many times shall I forgive my brother when he sins against me? Up to seven times?" Jesus answered, "I tell you, not seven times, but seventy-seven times?" Matthew 18:21,22 NIV.

When forgiveness ends, unforgiveness takes over. Unforgiveness is sin. God will not overlook it.

What if one refuses to forgive others for the wrongs received at their hands? He will receive no forgiveness from God. What is the consequence of not being forgiven by God? Jesus answered this question when he declared that the master "was wroth [with the unforgiving servant], and delivered him to the tormentors" Matthew 18:34.

What does it mean to be "delivered to the tormentors"? The Greek word for tormentor signifies one who imprisons and tortures. Through refusal to forgive, one puts himself under a curse. He is imprisoned in his own bitterness and demon spirits torture his mind, emotions and physical body.

3. **WITH HOPE.** Hope looks to the future with expectations of good. Hope refuses to be defeated by the miserable circumstances of the past and present. Hope for the Greeks meant comfort in distress. However, all hope is uncertain and deceptive except where its point of reference is God.

Hope is inseparably linked with trust. To hope is to trust. Hope is not a projection of what one can do for himself but a confidence in what God will do. Hope never rests upon controllable circumstances, but upon God. Hope is free of all anxiety when accompanied by a fear of God. Hope is the blessing of the righteous: "The hope of the righteous shall be gladness: but the expectation of the wicked shall perish" Proverbs 10:28.

Hope embraces patient endurance. Hence we must wait patiently, as did Abraham,

> Who against hope believed in hope, that he might become the father of many nations; according to that which was spoken, So shall thy seed be. Romans 4:18.

Abraham hoped on in faith when all human reason for hope was gone. This is the kind of hope that we must maintain when we are reaching for the comforting hand of God.

4. **WITH FAITH FOR INWARD HEALING NOW.** Faith brings hope to present reality. Faith sees the thing hoped for as already accomplished: "Now faith is being sure of what we hope for and certain of what we do not see" Hebrews 11:1 NIV.

It is marvelous to observe God at work in the lives of those who move in hope and faith. When people come to a deliverance or healing service simply knowing that God will touch them, the miracles of God flow abundantly. These people of faith make the minister look good, but he honestly knows that it was their faith that healed them.

Even Jesus was hindered in ministry when the people of His own community lacked faith: "And he could there do no mighty work, save that he laid his hands upon a few sick folk, and healed them" Mark 6:5.

Come to God in faith that He is there to meet you, and that He rewards those who seek Him sincerely and diligently.

5. **IN WILLINGNESS TO BE COMFORTED.** It is simple logic that if a person can choose NOT to be comforted, he can also choose to receive comfort. Where comfort is provided, it is a matter of meeting the conditions and accepting comfort. Willingness to be comforted is a decision. Comfort is the only remedy for a wounded spirit. God offers comfort for the wounded spirit.

Why would any sorrowful soul refuse to be comforted? In the next chapter we will search for reasons why some refuse comfort.

Chapter VIII

WHEN COMFORT IS REFUSED

Why do some hurting, tormented, sorrowing people sometimes refuse comfort? For the answer to this question let us re-examine those we have found in scripture who refused to be comforted.

WHY DID HANNAH
REFUSE COMFORT?

Hannah was barren, and nothing short of having a child would bring her solace.

Barrenness usually robbed a wife of her husband's affection; however, Elkana "loved Hannah", and showed her favoritism as over against his second wife, Peninnah, who had children. Elkana attempted to comfort Hannah by assuring her of his devotion:

> Hannah, why weepest thou? and why eatest thou not? and why is thy heart grieved? am not I better to thee than ten sons? I Samuel 1:8.

But, Hannah was not comforted by her husband's assurances of love. She refused all comfort. In her distress of heart, no other comfort was admissible as a substitute for childbearing.

It goes without saying that Elkanah was doing everything humanly possible to help Hannah conceive a child and to bring her cheer. However, human means were inadequate; only God could provide the comfort she sought.

Hannah was not looking to man for comfort but to God. After all, "the Lord had shut up her womb" I Samuel 1:5b. She pleaded with God in prayer with a sorrowful heart. Only God could comfort her, and the only answer she would accept from Him was to bear a child for His glory. Had not God promised...:

> If thou shalt hearken diligently unto the voice of the Lord thy God, to observe and to do all his commandments...Blessed shall be the fruit of thy body. Deuteronomy 28:1,4.

The writer of Hebrews, in chapter eleven, declared that there were more Old Testament examples of faith than he had time to mention. Hannah must be one of those unmentioned heroes of faith. She exhibited the same quality of faith as did Sarah of whom it is written:

> Through faith also Sarah herself received strength to conceive seed, and was delivered of a child when she was past age, because she judged him faithful who had promised. Hebrews 11:11.

WHY DID JACOB REFUSE COMFORT?

Jacob is another who, as we have noted, refused to be comforted. Why? He was living under the power of a lie. His sons caused him to believe that Joseph was dead — torn apart and devoured by a wild beast. Joseph was his favorite son. Joseph's mother was Rachael, his father's favorite wife, who had died as a result of complications from her second son's birth.

Jacob had seen the coat, torn and covered with blood. The evidence in his mind was conclusive: "Joseph is without doubt rent in pieces" Genesis 37:33b. Jacob believed wrongly, but he believed that Joseph had met a violent death and nothing remained for burial purposes. He completely discounted the supernatural dreams given to Joseph wherein God promised to exalt him in this life.

Humanly speaking, his grief was insurmountable. Nothing his family could say or do could change the facts as he saw them nor bring comfort to his broken heart.

Jacob was locked into his sorrow by a foolish vow. "And he said, I will go down into the grave unto my son mourning" Genesis 37:35b. He was snared by the words of his own mouth.

Others have followed Jacob in the same error. When a loved one dies the survivor declares that he will never be happy again. He vows to remain in perpetual sorrow. In his own mind his motivation may seem noble; done out of a sense of loyalty. Such vows are foolish; they are spoken curses which rob one of Divine comfort.

WHY DID "RACHAEL" REFUSE COMFORT?

The women of Israel, whom Jeremiah referred to as "Rachael", refused to be comforted when their sons became prisoners of war. Not even a small degree of comfort was brought to these mothers through Jeremiah's prophecy of a future restoration of the nation. Their sons were gone. Hopelessness consumed these grief-stricken mothers.

Matthew's gospel tells us that this weeping in Israel was prophetic of Herod's murdering all the children in Bethlehem and its environs in an attempt to kill the Christ child. Nevertheless, God's purposes were not frustrated. Jesus escaped Herod's sword that he might lay down His own life on the cross and be resurrected, thereby providing hope to all who die or lose loved ones through death.

The women of Israel remained in sorrow because they lacked hope of ever seeing their sons again. That is why Jeremiah preached hope to them.

> And there is hope in your future, says the Lord; your children shall come again to their own country. Jeremiah 31:17, Amplified Bible.

God still offers the hope of resurrection to all who sorrow and whose spirits are wounded through the death of others. Therefore...

> Sorrow not, even as others which have no hope. For if we believe that Jesus died and rose again, even so them also which sleep in Jesus will God bring with him. I Thessalonians 4:13,14.

Let none of us sorrow as though there is no tomorrow. Our hope is anchored in Him who conquered death and the grave.

WHY DID THE PSALMIST REFUSE COMFORT?

Psalm seventy-seven presents a man of God in a time of great, personal distress. The cause of pain is not disclosed, but once again we find one whose soul refuses to be comforted. The Hebrew word for "refused" literally means "to refuse with a resolved mind, which cannot be prevailed on by the means that have been used".[11]

This man's refusal to be comforted was not due to a lack of Divine resources but by an abject unwillingness to accept comfort.

His sorrow was kept alive and intensified by undisciplined thoughts and complaining. His comfort finally came about when he required his tormented mind to concentrate upon those things which are above. He determined within himself to "remember the works of the Lord"; all His works recorded in the Word from ancient times. The great and merciful acts of God became the center of his meditation. He found the route to comfort that leads through God's Word, for the Word led him into the abiding presence of "the God of all comfort" II Corinthians 1:3.

Undisciplined thought life leads the sorrowful soul into deep, dark valleys where despair takes over and all proffered comfort is rejected. But the spiritual mind, disciplined in meditation upon God's attributes and the truth of His Word bring the broken spirit to the Fountain of healing comfort.

---

11 Wilson, Wm. Old Testament Word Studies (1978), Grand Rapids, MI, Kregle Publications, p.344.

ADDITIONAL INSIGHTS

Hannah was comforted through faith in God. Jacob was comforted when he believed the evidence that Joseph still lived. Joseph being alive was to his father, Jacob, as great a revelation as the resurrection of The Lord Jesus Christ is to believers. "Rachael" was comforted through the revival of hope. Asaph was comforted through determined meditation upon the Word of God.

Through combining the various "keys" to comfort found through our study of these Old Testament patriarchs we have learned of the importance of hope, faith, assurance, and meditation upon the Word.

The Person of God is the common denominator in the combined formulas for comfort. Hope and faith are focused on God. Our assurance is in the Everlasting Father. Meditation upon the Word brings us into fellowship with God.

We must not become diverted from The God of Comfort in a quest for comfort elsewhere. Comfort is not dependent upon the reversal of adverse circumstances in life or the successful realization of life's dreams; comfort comes through one's resting in the bosom of the Comforter.

Comfort is a "grace" ministry. It is simply another facet of our salvation. We are saved by grace through faith; it is not of ourselves.[12] No man has ever attained salvation by successfully tugging at his own boot straps. The God of grace reaches down, and the heart of faith reaches up to receive His grace.

The grace of God extends to us with the gift of comfort just as it reaches out to us with the gift of eternal life, gifts of Divine healing and the gifts of the Holy Spirit's power. Comfort is a GIFT. We encounter comfort as we reach out to God in faith.

---

12 Ephesians 2:8,9.

Chapter IX

RECEIVE GOD'S COMFORT

Paul wrote to the church at Rome that, "Everyone who calls on the name of the Lord will be saved" Romans 10:12, NIV. The Greek word for "save", (sozo), means not only deliverance from sin but also deliverance from danger and suffering.

Paul explains that in order for one to call upon the Lord, he must first hear the gospel. God has called us and others to proclaim Jesus as Savior, Deliverer, Healer and Comforter. "As it is written, 'How beautiful are the feet of those who bring good news!'" Romans 10:15, NIV. For those able to discern the day of visitation, feet bearing "good news" have entered into your presence this very day!

Once the good news is proclaimed, it must be accepted. "But not all the Israelites accepted the good news. For Isaiah says, 'Lord, who has believed our message?'" Romans 19:16, NIV.

Who has believed the good news of Divine comfort?

Even Jeremiah, a messenger of comfort, refused to be comforted when his own prophecies began to be fulfilled. He who preached hope to "Rachael" at the loss of her children, balked at God's message of hope when he saw his nation devastated by war and multitudes carried into captivity.

Jeremiah, the weeping prophet, was in deep sorrow. God came to him and here is the conversation between Jehovah and Jeremiah:

Jeremiah: "Why is my pain perpetual, and my wound incurable, REFUSING TO BE HEALED? Will you indeed be to me as a deceitful brook, like waters that fail and are uncertain?" Jeremiah 15:18, emphasis mine.

Jeremiah's grief continued unabated. His wound seemed without remedy although God had promised a future restoration of the nation. The prophet's inner wound refused to be healed. He cried out to God in his complaint.

Jeremiah was wavering in his trust in God's goodness and power. He was afraid to trust God's Word for fear it would not come true, and his hopes would be dashed. Will God be to him as a deceitful brook?

This man of God compares himself to a traveler stranded in the desert. He is near death from dehydration when he sees a sparkling stream of water just ahead. Is it real, or is it a mirage? Dare Jeremiah trust in God's promise of comfort? If he approaches the river of Divine comfort will it vanish like a desert mirage?

Dear reader, have you ever been at that point in your life? Are you there today? Are you willing and able to trust God to comfort you NOW? Come to the waters of Divine comfort!

Jehovah: (Responding to Jeremiah's complaint): "Therefore thus says the Lord [to Jeremiah]. If you return [give up this mistaken tone of distrust and despair], then I will give you again a settled place of quiet and safety, and you shall be My minister" Jeremiah 13:19, Amplified Bible.

God challenges Jeremiah's attitude. Distrust and despair must be replaced with faith and hope, then he can appropriate God's comfort. Finally, Jeremiah, you can be God's minister!

When one has experienced God's comfort, he can comfort others. Since our own victory over sorrow through the comforting of our wounded spirits, we, our daughter and our friends, Steve and Linda Bell, have become ministers of comfort.

The blessings of receiving comfort and becoming a minister of comfort await all who sorrow.

> Praise be to the God and Father of our Lord Jesus Christ, the Father of compassion and the God of all comfort, who comforts us in all our troubles, so that we can

comfort those in any trouble with the comfort we ourselves have received from God. II Corinthians 1:3,4, NIV

Some are not comforted, not because they have refused comfort, but because they have never heard the good news that comfort is available. The "full gospel" includes not only the gift of eternal life, but also deliverance from demon spirits and the healing of the wounded spirit.

The comforting ministry of the Godhead is an often neglected part of the Gospel of Jesus Christ, of Whom it was written:

Surely He has borne our griefs — sickness, weakness and distress — AND CARRIED OUR SORROWS AND PAIN...He was wounded for our transgressions, He was bruised for our guilt and iniquities; the chastisement needful to obtain peace and well-being for us was upon Him, and with the stripes that wounded Him we are healed and made whole. Isaiah 53:4,5, Amplified Bible, emphasis mine.

The provision for our healing is in the atoning work of Christ. The cross purchased our redemption from sin, sickness and sorrow. Yes, Jesus' suffering provides healing for the wounded spirit: inner healing. "AND WITH HIS STRIPES WE ARE HEALED" Isaiah 53:2, emphasis mine.

Isaiah, chapter fifty-three, depicts Jesus as the suffering Servant. "He is DESPISED and REJECTED of men; a man of SORROWS, and acquainted with GRIEF" Isaiah 55:3, emphasis mine. He suffered in our stead — body, soul and spirit. We have no right to hold onto our sorrow and refuse His comfort — TO DO SO IS SIN!

Jesus agonized in the garden of Gethsemane saying, "My soul is exceeding sorrowful, even unto death". His last torturous words from the cross echoed across Calvary's hill, "My God, my God, why hast thou forsaken me?" Matthew 27:46. Shall He have suffered and sorrowed in vain?

Wherefore lift up the hands which hang down, and the feeble knees; And make straight paths for your feet, lest that which is lame be turned out of the way; but LET IT RATHER BE HEALED. Hebrews 12:12,13, emphasis mine.

Our sorrows make us weak, unable to lift up our hands in prayer and praise; they make us lame in our spiritual walk — crippled as with "feeble knees". "LET IT BE HEALED"! declares our Lord. "Let" speaks to the human will. "Let" addresses our responsibility before God. "Let" surrenders to Another's healing touch.

The Lord requires our response. We are brought to the point of decision and choice. Will we continue in our sorrow? Will we resolutely embrace our hurts? Is it not sin to refuse what Christ suffered to provide?

May the repentant heart cry out to God, "Oh, Lord, forgive me for stubbornly and foolishly holding on to rejection, hurt and grief. I have clung to that which you have borne for me through Your own suffering. Forgive me, Lord; cleanse me and comfort my wounded spirit".

"Looking diligently lest any man fail of the grace of God" Hebrews 12:15. The phrase, "fail of the grace of God", literally means, "fails to secure God's grace" Amplified Bible.

Comfort is a gift of God's grace. Choose to be comforted. "LET" the wound be healed. Let not Christ's suffering be in vain. Appropriate God's grace. Then you will affirm with the Psalmist:

> O Lord my God, I cried unto thee, and thou hast healed me. O Lord, thou hast brought up my soul from the grave....Thou hast turned for me my mourning into dancing: thou hast put off my sackcloth, and girded me with gladness. To the end that my glory [my soul] may sing praise to thee, and not be silent. Psalm 30:2,3,11,12, brackets mine.

Pray like this:

WARFARE PRAYER

Satan, I renounce you and all your works. I take back from you all the ground that I have ever yielded to you. You will not rob me of the comfort which Christ offers me. I resist you in the mighty name of The Lord Jesus Christ, and you are commanded to flee.

PRAYER

Heavenly Father, You know my life and all that has happened to me. You know the wounds that I have experienced at the hands of others and through life's adversities. I come to You with a forgiving heart. I willingly and completely forgive each person who has ever caused me pain and grief. I also forgive myself. I repent of all my sins and ask You to forgive and cleanse me by the precious blood of Jesus. I need the comfort of Your Holy Spirit. I refuse to hold on to the wounds which Christ bore for me through His own suffering and death. Take away my sorrow and give me Your peace and joy. I choose to be comforted, and I accept Your comforting touch — right now — in the Name of my Lord Jesus Christ.

AMEN!

Other Books By
Frank and Ida Mae Hammond

Pigs in the Parlor
Kingdom Living For the Family
The Saints At War (Spiritual Warfare Series, I)
Overcoming Rejection (Spiritual Warfare Series, II)
Demons and Deliverance in the Ministry of Jesus
(Spiritual Warfare Series, III)
Promoted By God
Our Warfare
Familiar Spirits
Soul Ties
God Warns America – Arise, Oh, Church

The Children's Bread Ministry
P.O. Box 789
Plainview, TX 79073